Commas
An Irreverent Primer

by Kate Ristau
and Maren Anderson

Contents

Introduction

You see the words *"Let's eat Grandpa,"* and you immediately think we are planning on feasting on Grandpa
tonight – spectacles and all. But, with one small **comma**, we can
save Grandpa's life:

- "Let's eat, Grandpa."

The first example promotes cannibalism. The second promotes
communal dining. It might just be me, but I prefer the second
one. I kind of like Grandpa.

If you are like Grandpa and me, and not a cannibal, you probably learned some very important ideas during your Freshman
year in high school. If you really are like Grandpa and me, you
promptly forgot them all. Especially the stuff about commas.

The only idea that stuck with Grandpa and me is that you put
a comma where you breathe.

X When I saw Grandpa [breath], my eyes filled with tears [breath], tears of disbelief [breath], that someone [breath], that anyone [breath], would think about feasting [breath], on that dear old man.

Did I mention that I suffer from a little bit of asthma? And that Grandpa is really old?

There's something not right about that idea that we should put commas where we breathe. Something that would make my poor, underappreciated Freshman English teacher Mrs. Orton scream (I can barely type over the sound of her voice).

And here it is: commas follow rules. And to know where to put them, we gotta know the rules.

I can already hear you screaming: "But there are too many rules! And grammar is so boring!"

Will you and Mrs. Orton ever leave me alone?

Listen, what you've got in your hands should make all those comma rules a lot easier to understand. This is a primer – a simple, irreverent one at that. It will not teach you pronouns and gerunds and indirect objects (besides, you only really need to know indirect objects if you plan on learning Spanish or if you hate being direct).

This primer will most likely bend a lot of other grammar rules along the way, but if you read it, and pay attention, you might learn how to avoid cannibalism.

By the way, this is why I am compelled to put a black "**X**" next to the examples in this book that are *wrong*. I can't help it. It's what I do.

So, let's begin.

The Basics

B efore we get too far into this, we need to establish some basic ideas. Stay with me, it won't hurt (at least not like the emotional pain of eating your family members).

First, every sentence has two parts: a subject and a predicate.

The **subject** is who or what the sentence is about – the main idea.

For example:

- Grammar tastes like belly button lint.

In that sentence, **grammar** is the subject. That sentence is about grammar and its...flavorfulness.

Subjects can get more complicated, but let's just stick with that for right now.

The second part of a sentence, the **predicate**, tells us something about that subject, like if it is running or happy or flavorful. In the above example, the predicate is "tastes like belly button lint."

Simple, right?

If you've ever had your boss or Mrs. Orton tell you that you are using too many sentence fragments, they are basically saying that your sentence is missing a subject or a predicate: it's not a complete sentence.

Take this example:

X Rocks my face off.

Yeah, it does! Now...what rocks your face off? You're missing a subject, Brosef. That's a **sentence fragment**.

But, this is a comma primer. Go learn that somewhere else.

Commas and Independent Clauses

Alright, we know about subjects and predicates, we understand what grammar tastes like, and we've decided to hold off on eating Grandpa. Good. Let's take our new knowledge and apply it to commas.

Our first taste of commas has to do with **independent clauses.**

I know—you're falling asleep already. But give independent clauses a chance! They are like the filling part of our belly button lint.

That **metaphor** is getting really gross.

Moving on, an independent clause is a phrase that can stand on its own. You could yell it across the room at me, and I would be like, "Yeah, that totally made sense what you just said about unicorns."

In other words, and with more unicorns, an independent clause has both a subject and a predicate. It can be its own cute little sentence. Example:

- Unicorns have horns.

That's an independent clause. It has a subject (unicorns) and that subject is doing or being something (having horns).

That's a simple independent clause. We could pretty it up a bit:

- Malaysian unicorns, as opposed to Sri Lankan unicorns, have dazzling, rainbowlicious horns.

You weren't supposed to learn anything from that last example. I just wanted to write it.

What does all this have to do with commas? Simple. If I have two independent clauses, and I want to connect them, I can't just put a comma there. That's called a **comma splice** even though commas *cannot* splice sentences together. Unicorns, and Mrs. Orton, really hate that.

X Malaysian unicorns are rainbowlicious, Sri Lankan unicorns are sparkly.

Geez, now Mrs. Orton and the unicorns are screaming. That comma does not belong there.

Here's why. If you have two independent clauses (two complete ideas), and you want them to hang out together, you need to add a **coordinating conjunction**; you can't just add a comma.

A conjunction is a cute little connector word like: **For, And, Nor, But, Or, Yet,** and **So** (They spell **FANBOYS**!). The FAN-BOYS bring independent clauses together. And trust me, if you want to bring Malaysian unicorns and Sri Lankan unicorns together, you better have a FANBOY. Here's a FANBOY in action:

- Malaysian unicorns are rainbowlicious, and Sri Lankan unicorns are sparkly.

Sweet. You used a comma and one of the FANBOYS. You are rocking my face off, Grandpa eater.

You could also take out the FANBOY, break that sentence in two, and the unicorns would still get along just fine.

- Malaysian unicorns are rainbowlicious. Sri Lankan unicorns are sparkly.

That sentence totally sparkles. This one doesn't:

X Malaysian unicorns are sparkly, and so very rainbowlicious.

That doesn't work, and not just because of your blatant misunderstanding of the unicorn species. You should only put a comma with your conjunction if you have two independent clauses. Each clause must be able to stand on its own. Sadly, "so very rainbowlicious" is not an independent clause. It is not a complete idea.

Please don't put a comma there (think of the unicorns). Here are some examples to drive our last few points home:

- Unicorns are filled with pudding or guts.

No commas – that second part is not a complete idea.

X   That unicorn is planning on taking over the world, and instituting Free Pie Day.

Take that comma out. Instituting Free Pie Day, though a worthy endeavor, is not an independent clause – it can't stand on its own.

• I believe in lollipops, and she believes in the apocalypse.

Hey! Two independent clauses, joined by a comma and conjunction! Good work!

X   She is a bit depressing, or maybe doesn't like thinking long term.

No subject after that conjunction, right? No comma, then!

Unicorns and lollipops aside, the basic idea is this: you should put a comma before a conjunction that is connecting two independent clauses.

Do it for the unicorns.

Commas in a List

In case you were confused about independent clauses, or don't particularly care about unicorns (you black-hearted cannibal), I'll take it easy and talk to you about something you probably already know about: commas in a series.

This rule is simple: if you have a list, separate the ideas in the series with commas.

X   Onions mushrooms and potatoes are all not beans.

You need to separate those items!

•   Onions, mushrooms, and potatoes are all not beans.

Wait, hold the rainbows. There's a disruption in the unicorn pasture. Spangle said you don't need that comma after mushrooms. Twinklefoot disagreed, pawed her in the face, and told her to follow the rules and separate those ideas.

Who's right?

In a sense, they're both right. But, for reasons we will explore, I'm going to side with Twinklefoot.

Some unicorns, like Spangle, don't put that comma (often called the "**Oxford Comma**," after all of those British unicorns) before the conjunction ("and") at the end of the series. Spangle would write:

- Onions, mushrooms and potatoes are all not beans.

But Spangle is just lazy.* And, oftentimes, he confuses other unicorns. For example, Spangle might say:

X   I like eating turkey, tofu, ham and cheese sandwiches.

Does that mean Spangle likes ham and cheese sandwiches? Or ham sandwiches and cheese sandwiches? That gets an **X** for being ambiguous.

This is more important than you think. Sandwiches are magic. Giving a unicorn the right sandwich can make the difference between rainbow sparkles and psycho-killing.

So, to avoid the confusion (and the psycho-killing), use the Oxford comma. Not for the unicorns this time. For yourself.

There is a noteable style exception here. If you are a journalist, the Associated Press Stylebook suggests you don't use the Oxford Comma, unless it's absolutely necessary. Of course, all journalists are cannibals and can't be trusted, anyway. They are also horrible at ordering sandwiches.

Commas after Introductory Phrases

If you gave Rainbowlegs the right sandwich, odds are you're still with us, and you're just in time for commas after introductory words.

The basic rule here: Use a comma after introductory words at the beginning of the sentence. In other words, when you have some stuff at the beginning of your sentence, before the sentence itself really starts kicking, that stuff needs to be separated with a comma. This applies to **dependent clauses** at the beginning of the sentence and transition words, too.

Let's start with those dependent clauses. Basically, a dependent clause can't stand on its own.

For example:

X   When Dr. Who arrived.

Can that sentence stand on its own? Nope. It leaves us waiting and wanting more. For gosh sakes, what *happened* when Dr. Who arrived? That dependent clause is not telling us. It's an incomplete idea.

My mom (an eighth grade English teacher) tells me I can immediately tell if a clause is dependent by employing this helpful acronym: **AAAWWUBBIS** (Awoooooobis). I told her that wasn't a very helpful acronym, but she wouldn't let it go. She told me to write them down for you.

As	When	If
After	Until	Since
Although	Before	
While	Because	

Don't worry. If you can't remember that super-helpful acronym, you have the list of words right up there. Sweet! Am I right? Thanks, Mom.

AAAWWUBBIS words are subordinating conjunctions. Use them, and suddenly all the words they are with become dependent on the rest of the sentence – they become a dependent clause. Note: if you use an AAWWUBBIS word and do not have a "rest of the sentence," you're writing a sentence fragment. Stop that, you loser.

Anyway, enough about you. Use a comma at the end of that dependent clause and you're doing it right. For example:

- When Dr. Who arrived, the mannequins were trying to strangle Rose.

In that sentence, *when* is our AAAWWUBBIS word. The main part of the sentence is about murder-minded mannequins. We have a comma after *arrived* because that is where the dependent clause ends.

Get it? Commas go after dependent clauses (phrases that are incapable of going anywhere on their own) at the beginning of sentences.

16

- Although the plastic ooze had literally consumed her boyfriend, Rose was still in a pretty good mood.

Yay! Comma after the dependent clause that starts with *although* – our AAAWWUBBIS word of the day! Cupcakes for everyone.

X   If it had been me I would have been a little ticked.

No cupcakes for you, Kin-Eater. That sentence starts with one of our AAAWWUBBIS words, so it has a dependent clause at the beginning. There should be a comma before the real meat of the sentence begins (before the subject, which is "I").

- If it had been me, I would have been a little ticked.

Here's a twist, though. If you flip that sentence, and your AAWWUBBIS word is in the middle, you don't need that comma:

- I would have been a little ticked if it had been me.

Both versions of this sentence are grammatically correct. But remember, if you have the AAAWWUBBIS word at the beginning, you need that comma. If it is in the middle of the sentence, you don't.

Unless you're Dr. Who. Then you can do whatever you want.

17

Commas and Transitions

You should also use a comma after other little intro words, clauses, and phrases. A good example of these types of words is a **transition**. Transitions form a bridge between sentences or within a sentence. Some common transitions include: also, on the other hand, however, and then.

Google "transition words" and you'll get tons of them. Google "my cat likes bananas" and you'll get a YouTube video of a cat eating a banana. I'm not comfortable with this.

Before you get lost on YouTube for several hours, let's look at some examples.

- Of course, the cat enjoyed his feast.

Good job putting that comma after that transition.

X However she made a total mess.

How many times do I have to tell you? Put a comma after that transition, nerdburger.

- However, she made a total mess.

"But wait," you say, "Spangle says I don't need those commas. Spangle says that if I have a short intro phrase or transition, I don't have to use the tools of the Devil."

Darn you, Spangle.

Okay guys, Spangle is right. You don't have to with those short introductory phrases. And some writers don't. They're total losers, but hey, you can do what you want.

Just know that it is never wrong if you put a comma after an intro phrase or transition, and it might get confusing if you don't.

Quick note: whatever you choose to do, stay consistent within your paper. There is nothing more disgusting than an author who sometimes uses a comma after a short transition and sometimes doesn't.

Well, except maybe a cat eating a banana. That is really disgusting.

Commas and Nonrestrictive Clauses

You know what's not disgusting? Commas and **nonrestrictives**. They're downright **righteous**.

Don't get so agitated. Nonrestrictives are very easy to understand.

A nonrestrictive is a phrase, clause or idea that you could delete from the sentence, and it wouldn't matter. It wouldn't change the meaning of the sentence. Nonrestrictives can also be called nonessential. They are not essential to the function of the sentence. The party can go on without them.

The rule is that if you have a nonrestrictive in the middle of your sentence, you should put some commas around it. For example:

- The Unicorn Convention of 1876, the year Old Bud died, was downright righteous.

Now, I could easily take out "the year Old Bud died." That stuff is nonessential. It is a nonrestrictive clause. It is not restricting me from doing anything (except being depressed...poor Old Bud).

Nonrestrictives can be in the middle, end, or beginning of a sentence. They can be big ideas or even just a couple of words. If you have a restrictive clause at the end of your sentence, you should put a comma at the start and a period where it ends. That's how you let us know it's nonessential.

- I believe in elves, which are tiny woodland creatures.

"Which are tiny woodland creatures" is not essential to the sentence. It tells us something important about your deep understanding of elven culture, but it is not necessary.

X I watched the elf, who was screaming at my fat fingers.

Why do you have that comma there? We need to know what that elf is doing. That is essential to our sentence. Stop it with that comma. Seriously. You're making me mad.

That elf would be mad too. Elves are not delightful little creatures. They will bite your finger off, your delicious fat finger, if you forget to set off parenthetical information with a comma.

Don't know what that means? Let me explain.

Just like nonrestrictives, if you have stuff that horns in on the flow of the sentence, you should put some commas around it. Take this unicorn example:

- Fluffy Wondercakes, despite his name, is a bit hard around the edges.

See how that phrase "despite his name" just kind of snuck in there? Horned on in? Disrupted everything? You should put commas around that insolent phrase.

X Elves unlike unicorns have a propensity for random breakdancing.

What part of that sentence felt like it was horning its way in? The unicorn part, right? They always do that. Try this sentence instead:

- Elves, unlike unicorns, have a propensity for random breakdancing.

There. That's better. Always put commas around info that interrupts the sentence or is not essential to the sentence.

Or else, hide your delicious fingers.

Ristau & Anderson

Commas and Quotes

If you still have all of your fingers, you're probably ready for some more comma goodness. If you lost one, you're probably bleeding profusely. Go to the Emergency Room before the elves start playing EMT.

Seriously. Run. They're not very good at it.

As for ye intact noble maidens and fair knights, onto quotes forthwith.

If quotation marks ("like these") had it their way, they would hug the filling out of everything. They really love filling.

Nevertheless, they only have situational hugging power. Don't worry, though. They can definitely hug on commas. They always hug on commas.

What's that? You need a unicorn example? Okay. Just for you over there in the pink.

- "Sparklepuss is the floweriest unicorn ever," cried Pansy.

See how the quotation marks are like giant arms embracing all of that quote? That's how they work. They are a big warm, fuzzy **sasquatch** encircling the quotation with their manly scent.

X   "Oh, Barnacles! I wish my dragon had even a tenth of that mojo", grumbled the illiterate troll.

What are you even doing? Why would you think those quotation marks would just leave that comma out in the cold, alone and shivering? What are you—some kind of monster? Be a gentleman, and put the quotes around that punctuation mark, you **troll**.

- "Oh, Barnacles! I wish my dragon had even a tenth of that mojo," grumbled the illiterate troll.

That's much better. Check out this one too:

- "Oliver was crushed, quite literally," Meliferous said.

See where that comma went? Inside the quotes. Getting all hugged and stuff. That's where it belongs.

One of the reasons for putting that comma where it gets some love is really, really neat—for typographical nerds like me. You know, the type of people who think the words "em (m) dash" and "en (n) dash" are cooler than "dash" and "hyphen." But, I digress.

The story I heard is that back when printers had to carve letters by hand, the period and comma were so small that they would break off. So, any time the printers could, they would stick something on the other side—like quotation marks.

So, an irrelevant, archaic reason now governs the way we use a comma.

The sasquatch is fine with that. He loves himself some filling.

"I hope you in the pink are happy now," he said.

Commas and Coordinate Adjectives

B arry Manticore is outside serenading his girlfriend, Mildred, with his trumpet-voice, entertaining everyone in the neighborhood except Charlene Chupacabra, who is itchy and grouchy all the time.

- "Barry! Your singing is loud and obnoxious. Stop that loud, obnoxious singing!" cries Charlene.

- "Go scratch your sharp red spikes," Barry sings back. "Ha, ha! You have sharp red spikes!"

Man, these two don't like each other very much, do they? But they demonstrate that the best insults are usually strings of **adjectives.**

I know. You're screaming again. Adjectives? What are those? Let's go back to the basics one more time.

First off: **nouns.** In a sentence, a noun is a person, place, thing, idea, or animal.

Take this sentence:

- A manticore has a human head, a lion body, and a scorpion tail.

The noun in that sentence is manticore, which is a frightening animal. There are lots of different types of nouns, but shut-up. Who cares? On to adjectives.

Adjectives describe nouns or pronouns. They can tell you if a chupacabra is itchy, smart, or grouchy. In fact, all of these adjectives can be used to accurately describe chupacabras.

You have probably noticed that sometimes you use more than one adjective to describe a noun, like Charlene did when she described Barry's voice. But here's the issue: sometimes you need to use a comma to separate those adjectives, and sometimes you don't. It all seems pretty random, too, doesn't it?

Well, it's not. Don't think that. There is method to the manti-core and chupacabra madness. Let's look at those insults again:

- "Barry! Your singing is loud and obnoxious. Stop that loud, obnoxious singing!" cries Charlene.

- "Go scratch your sharp red spikes," Barry sings back. "Ha, ha! You have sharp red spikes!"

So, why is there a comma between "loud" and "obnoxious" but not between "sharp" and "red"? That's because "loud" and "obnoxious" are **coordinate adjectives**, while "sharp" and "red" are **cumulative adjectives**. You need commas between lists of coordinate adjectives but not between clumps of cumulative adjectives.

Fine, but how do you tell the difference?

Think of coordinate adjectives as equals (the "co" part of the word means "equal"). They modify the same word in the same way. Sometimes, they even describe the same quality. You can think of the commas as living in a list of equal adjectives.

"How can I tell if the adjectives are equal?" you ask. Well, don't ask the manticore, that's all I have to say. He'll break into a fanfare, and you'll never get him to shut up. Not that you'll get an answer from the chupacabra, either. She's likely to just snap at you.

That's why we're here.

Let's take those and re-write them.

- "Barry! Your singing is obnoxious and loud. Stop that obnoxious, loud singing!" cries Charlene.

X   "Go scratch your red sharp spikes," Barry sings back. "Ha, ha! You have red sharp spikes!"

Look at that! One of those adjective pairs works great, but the other is as clunky as a Muzak version of "Mandy." What happened? Well, the first pair is an example of coordinate adjectives (equal adjectives) while the second is a pair of cumulative adjectives (building adjectives).

How do I know? I have two secret tests for finding coordinate adjectives:

Test #1: *Reverse the order of the adjectives. If they still work, they are coordinates and need a comma between them.*

- "Barry! Your singing is obnoxious and loud. Stop that obnoxious, loud singing!" cries Charlene.

X "Go scratch your red sharp spikes," Barry sings back. "Ha, ha! You have red sharp spikes!"

"Obnoxious, loud" or "loud, obnoxious"? Makes no real difference. Both adjectives are describing the same quality (the sound) of singing, so you can mix them up and not lose any meaning.

However, "red sharp spikes" sounds worse than "sharp red spikes." Why? These are cumulative adjectives. Without getting too technical (you just want to know where the comma goes, not get a degree in linguistics), you can't change the order of adjectives that describe different parts of a noun, like size, and color, and sharpness. They are building upon each other in a particular order. In this case, we need to know how sharp the spikes are before we know what color they are. So, no comma.

On to the next test.

Test #2: *Insert an "and" between the adjectives. If they still work, they are coordinates and need a comma between them.*

- "Barry! Your singing is loud and obnoxious. Stop that loud and obnoxious singing!" cries Charlene.

X "Go scratch your sharp and red spikes," Barry sings back. "Ha, ha! You have sharp and red spikes!"

Loud and obnoxious singing? That works. Put a comma between your coordinate adjectives.

Sharp and red spikes? I can hear Charlene judging you from here. No comma between your cumulative adjectives.

Now let's look at how those four-legged insult-tossers used commas at the beginning of this section:

- "Barry! Your singing is loud and obnoxious. Stop that loud, obnoxious singing!" cries Charlene.

- "Go scratch your sharp red spikes," Barry sings back. "Ha, ha! You have sharp red spikes!"

See how they use commas or "and" between the coordinate (equal) adjectives but not between the cumulative adjectives? That's some good insulting, my friends. Take it from Barry and Charlene; if you want to double up your insults, think about where you put your commas.

Ristau & Anderson

Commas and Direct Address

A lright. Enough with the insults. Remember your spikey grammar dragon, Meliferous?

Grammar dragons can be super-helpful. Trust me.

But, here's the thing. Meliferous has a habit of impaling your lunch on his spiney behind and parading around the fire-pit with your peanut butter and jelly sandwich.

And you're fed up. Seriously. You're hungry. So, let's say that you finally work up the nerve, and you corner Meliferous. He then promptly sits down on your rainbowlicious sandwich and refuses to move.

This is NOT good.

Let's review how you might write a note to appease your grammar dragon.*

Please note that all requests made to grammar dragons need to be put in writing.

Let's say you tried this approach:

X   Meliferous get your pointy bottom off of my peanut butter and jelly.

Unfortunately for you, this would result in more than your sandwich becoming all toasty and gooey. Why? You did not put a comma after Meliferous's name, as you need to after a **direct address**.

Direct address is when you talk directly to someone in your sentence. Simple, am I right? Yeah, I am. Trust me.

Take, for example, what you just wrote to Meliferous. You need a comma after "Meliferous." This is because you are talking directly to him:

• Meliferous, get your pointy bottom off of my peanut butter and jelly.

Just like those nonrestrictives, a direct address is nonessential. The information can be removed without changing the meaning of the sentence.

Confused? Think about that time your mom was really mad at you because you let your grammar dragon melt the carpet in front of the T.V. Remember what she said?

• "Agamemnon, you get your grammar dragon out of here before I unleash the style demon on your skinny behind!"

Man, she was so mad. She didn't even have to say your name. She could have left it out. She could have said:

- "Get your grammar dragon out of here before I unleash the style demon on your skinny behind!"

But she used your name. Your full name. That's when you knew you were in trouble, dude.

And, yes, it was useless to point out to your Mom that your grammar dragon simply sneezed on accident. Your Mom wouldn't even listen. She's not up for negotiation.

Luckily, your grammar dragon is. But you have to, you know, use the right grammar. Before we get to the right grammar, let's take a look at a couple more notes that would have resulted in Meliferous sizzling the clothes right off your body:

X   Get your pointy bottom off of my peanut butter and jelly Meliferous.

X   Did you know Meliferous that your pointy bottom is on my peanut butter and jelly?

Direct address needs to be set off from the sentence with commas, no matter where in the sentence it occurs: front, back, Middle Ages, wherever.

Here are a couple of grammatically correct ways to write that note:

- Get your pointy bottom off of my peanut butter and jelly, Meliferous.

- Did you know, Meliferous, that your pointy bottom is on my peanut butter and jelly?

Notice in the last example that Meliferous is set off front and back by commas? Good. Do that and your grammar dragon won't crisp you up.

So, now you know how to write a note that Meliferous the grammar dragon will be well pleased to receive and will not result in her burning up your lunch…or you.

I can't do all the work here, though. You'll still gotta work on saying that nicer. Grammar dragons are sensitive creatures, after all.

Some Random Extra Commas

If you're still trying to convince Meli to get off your sandwich, you're probably starving by now. Don't worry; there are a couple of other little rules I'll throw at you, then we're done—and so are my candy corn waffles. I might even share them with you.

Get your syrup out while we finish up.

First, don't use a comma after *such, as,* or *like.* That's not cool. You don't need that comma. An example would be if you said something like this sentence. The one you just read. See how there was not a comma after the word *like*? That's good. I'm good. Thanks for noticing.

Second, don't use a comma if you already have a question mark or exclamation point. That's just stupid.

"Why do people do that?" you might be thinking.

I honestly do not know. They are losers. Don't grow up to be like them. They would write something like this:

X   "Am I a loser?," she asked.

These losers also ask a lot of questions. You'll know them by their question marks and excess commas. Beware!

Third, because I am numbering these miscellaneous uses, you should use commas with places and addresses, but don't go crazy.

Three *not crazy* examples:

- The smell of trolls delights the senses of people who live in Geneseo, Illinois.

Remember to separate towns/cities/rural hamlets and states with a comma.

- If you have a complaint about this book, send it to Donut Care, 12345 S. Unicorn Way, Precipice, Oregon, 12345.

See those commas? That's good stuff. Yeah, baby.

Fourth, and finally, take a deep whiff of those waffles as we finish up by talking about dates. This is the easy part. You've seen a date before, right? Take this:

- My dragon was born on April 8, 1954, in a volcano.

See where I put the comma? After the day and the year? That's good.

Don't do this:

X   My dragon was born on April, 8 1954 in a volcano.

Or this:

X   My dragon was born on April 8 1954 in a volcano.

38

Why would you do that?

Stop that.

However, if you are British, in the military, or just really hate commas, you can write your date like this: 8 April 1954.

That's perfect. No commas. I hate them anyway.

Conclusion

So, that's it. The basic stuff you need to know about commas. If you are a total nerd, like me, I've given you an exercise to work through on the next page. If you are confused about any words or want to know how to define "troll," check out the index. If you could give a fart less, well, I didn't want you here in the first place.

For the rest of you, well done. I can see a bright future ahead of you. One full of unicorns, dragons, elves, and the taste of waffles in your mouth.

Maybe Grandpa will even join you at the dinner table. He's looking a little thin.

Give him a waffle. It's the least you can do, you cannibal.

Exercises

Exercise 1: Independent clauses and FANBOYS

FANBOYS are coordinating conjunctions. You can use them to connect independent clauses together...as long as you add a comma. The FANBOYS are For, And, Nor, But, Or, Yet, and So.

Example: I rock ___ and she is a literal rock.

Answer: I rock, and she is a literal rock.

Explanation: "I rock" is a complete sentence with a subject and predicate. "She is a literal rock" is a complete sentence with a subject and predicate, too. If I want to put them together, I have to add one of the FANBOYS (in this case, I use "and"), and then I add a comma. Just putting the comma there does not rock. That would be a comma splice.

Directions: Add commas below as needed. Do not subtract commas. Unless you have white-out. Then, I guess I can't stop you.

1. Geology rocks ___ and chemistry does not rock.

2. Folklorists are pretty ___ and smart.

3. Your mom called ___ and she said you should stop talking.

4. Tom stopped by ___ and couldn't find you. I told him you were abducted by aliens ___ and he was surprisingly okay with it.

5. I don't have any syrup ___ so you shouldn't eat those waffles. Okay, I lied. There's syrup ___ but I don't want you eating my waffles.

Now, check out the word search below and see how many FANBOYS you can find.

```
O X O K X F Q
F U B V S O A
D G U P R R M
B N T J O T M
O N A B P E O
T P O F O Y C
S C Y R R O W
```

Exercise 2: Lists

If you have a list of more than two items, you are going to need a comma to separate the words in that list. Some people argue that you do not need the final comma in the list (often referred to as the Oxford comma or the serial comma). But, in many cases, it makes the list less ambiguous or confusing.

Exercises

Example: For breakfast, the dragon eats eggs ___ peasants ___ and kings.

Answer: For breakfast, the dragon eats eggs, peasants, and kings.

Explanation: With no comma after peasants, we are unsure if the dragon is enjoying a nice scramble of peasants and kings, or if she is enjoying them separately.

Directions: In the time traveler's speech below, the dragon ate all of the Oxford Commas. He does not like them. To spite him, put them all back in.

Loyal lords, ladies and noble guests, it is my great honor

to be with you today. I have traveled through time and space to

arrive in your beautiful, lovely and awe-inspiring land. I have

battled orcs, goblins and fairy kings. I have slain them all. I

stand before you today with but one wish in my tired, lonely and

humble heart. Please, do not eat me.

Exercise 3: Introductory phrases and transitions

If you have a dependent clause, a transition, or an introductory phrase at the beginning of a sentence, you need to separate it from the rest of the sentence with a comma. In other words, if there's stuff at the beginning of your sentence, before the sentence really starts, it should be set off with a comma. It's easy to identify dependent clauses at the beginning of a sentence because they often start with an AAAWWUBBIS word. AAAWWUBBIS words are subordinating conjunctions like **As**, **After**, **Although**, **While**, **When**, **Until**, **Before**, **Because**, **If**, and **Since**. If you have an AAAWWUBBIS word at the beginning of your sentence, you know you're going to need a comma after that clause. But, if you have an AAAWWUBBIS word in the middle of a sentence, you won't need that comma.

> Example: When your mom called ___ I told her you went to Candy Mountain with those unicorns.
>
> Answer: When your mom called, I told her you went to Candy Mountain with those unicorns.

Explanation: "When" is one of our AAAWWUBBIS words, so I know I am going to need a comma at the end of that first clause.

Directions: Read the examples below. Decide where you would put commas. Fill the blanks with those commas. For extra points, use green ink.

1. When I told her where you went ___ your mom was a little worried.

2. The liopleurodon hasn't been giving good directions to Candy Mountain ___ since he had that surgery.

3. The Magical Bridge of Hope and Wonder has also been closed ___ because of renovations.

4. Clearly ___ it's just not a good idea ___ to go to Candy Mountain.

Exercise 4: Nonrestrictives and parentheticals

Nonrestrictives and parentheticals are those little phrases you can delete from your sentence, and the sentence will still work. You have to put commas around those little phrases to prevent them from escaping and attacking the rest of the sentence.

Example: Fairies ___ little creatures with wings ___ are not ghosts.

Answer: Fairies, little creatures with wings, are not ghosts.

Explanation: *Little creatures with wings* is a nonrestrictive phrase. We could take it out of the sentence and the fairies would go on not being ghosts. There is no impact on the sentence.

Part 1 Directions: There are two columns below. The left side is full of complete sentences. The right side is a list of nonrestrictive phrases. Match the nonrestrictive phrase on the left to its complete sentence on the right to fancy up that sentence. The first one has been completed for you.

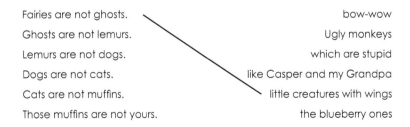

Fairies are not ghosts.	bow-wow
Ghosts are not lemurs.	Ugly monkeys
Lemurs are not dogs.	which are stupid
Dogs are not cats.	like Casper and my Grandpa
Cats are not muffins.	little creatures with wings
Those muffins are not yours.	the blueberry ones

Part 2 Directions: Now, fill in the blanks below. Remember, you should put commas around those disruptive phrases.

1. Fairies _____

    _____ are not ghosts.

2. Ghosts _____

    _____ are not lemurs.

3. Lemurs _____

    _____ are not dogs.

4. Dogs _____

    _____ are not cats.

5. Cats _____

    _____ are not muffins.

6. Those muffins _____

    _____ are not yours.

Exercise 5: Quotes

Commas go inside quotation marks, not outside. Keep them inside the warm, fuzzy embrace of those quotation marks, you sasquatch.

Example: "Oranges are red ___ " ___ Dum-dum said.

Answer: "Oranges are red, " Dum-dum said.

Explanation: The comma goes inside the quote. Do you really need an explanation? Were you even paying attention?

Directions: In the exercises below, destroy the sentences where the commas are somewhere weird. For extra credit, add in three unicorns.

1. "The oranges are a beautiful shade of burgundy", Dum-dum said.

2. "No, they are not," I said.

3. "Yes, they are", Dum-Dum said.

4. "Don't be a sludgeface," I said.

5. "Just look at them", said Dum-Dum. "Those are magical oranges."

6. "Oh", I said. "What makes them magical?"

7. "They're red,".

Exercise 6: Direct address

Direct address is when you talk to someone directly in your sentence. Just like a nonrestrictive or a parenthetical, you need to set it off from the sentence with a comma.

Example: If you eat my candy corn waffles ___ Meg ___ I will tell the pixies.

Answer: If you eat my candy corn waffles, Meg, I will tell the pixies.

Explanation: I am talking directly to Meg. I do not really need her name in there, so I put commas around it. I put it in there because she is a thief, and I don't trust her.

Directions: Insert commas into the exercise below. Do not insert commas where there should not be commas. That won't work.

1. You know how the pixies feel about stealing ___ Meg ___.

2. I mean ___ Meg ___ do you even remember what happened last time?

3. Meg ___ they made you drink maple syrup for seven years.

4. That was almost as terrible as that movie ___ Seven Years in Tibet.

5. You're right ___ Meg ___; Brad Pitt did make that movie a little better.

6. But please ___ for the love of butter ___ stop stealing my candy corn waffles.

Exercise 7: Coordinate adjectives

Coordinate adjectives are equals. They modify the same word in the same way. So, we put a comma between them. Cumulative adjectives are not equal. They build off of each other. You can tell if you need the comma between your adjectives by doing the little manticore test:

If you flip them, does the sentence still work? You need the comma.

If you put an "and" between them, does the sentence still work? Add that comma.

Example: That is one shiny ___ red apple.

Answer: That is one shiny red apple.

Explanation: Shiny and red are not equal. They build off each other. Check out the sentence if I do the test: That is one red shiny apple. Icky, right? That just sounds weird. And if I do the second test, I get this: That is one shiny and red apple. It feels like we don't need that "and," right? That's how we know they're cumulative adjectives, and that we don't need that comma.

Directions: You have decided to pursue employment in the Magical Property Division of Carry Motter Enterprises. Before you will be considered for a position, you must first fill out the personal profile below. Decide what words to use based on whether or not there is a comma between the adjectives. Remember, if there's a comma, the words are coordinate – they are equal (like tasty, gratifying). If there's no comma, the words are cumulative – they mean something different (like small brown).

1. I ride a _____ , _____ broomstick.

2. I own _____ _____

   _____ owls.

3. I make _____ , _____ Nutter Beer.

4. I wish I owned a _____ _____ hippogriff.

Exercise 8: Random commas

Directions: Fill in the blanks and add your commas too. Use the rules we discussed, and you too will one day become a dragon.

When I went to the _____ I bought a box of
(place)

_____. Clearly they were made by
(food)

_____ and not intended for
(fantastical creatures)

human consumption. The cashier warned me "Bro

that stuff's nasty." But I did not _____ and I
(synonym of listen)

feasted on them _____.
(adverb (word ending in -ly))

They tasted like _____
(adjective (describe-y word))

_____ and _____.
(adjective)   (adjective)

On May _____ 2015 I died of _____.
(number)   (horrible disease)

That day a very _____ day indeed was the end of
(adjective)

my existence as a human. That's cool though. Now I'm

a _____.
(fantastical creature)

Answers

Exercise 1 Answers

1. Geology rocks, and chemistry does not rock.
2. Folklorists are pretty and smart.
3. Your mom called and she said you should stop talking.
4. Tom stopped by and couldn't find you. I told him you were abducted by aliens, and he was surprisingly okay with it.
5. I don't have any syrup, so you shouldn't eat those waffles. Okay, I lied. There's syrup, but I don't want you eating my waffles.

Exercise 2 Answers

Loyal lords, ladies, and noble guests, it is my great honor to be with you today. I have traveled through time and space to arrive in your beautiful, lovely, and awe-inspiring land. I have battled orcs, goblins, and fairy kings. I have slain them all. I stand before you today with but one wish in my tired, lonely, and humble heart. Please, do not eat me.

Exercise 3 Answers

1. When I told her where you went, your mom was a little worried.

2. The liopleurodon hasn't been giving good directions to Candy Mountain since he had that surgery.
3. The Magical Bridge of Hope and Wonder has also been closed because of renovations.
4. Clearly, it's just not a good idea to go to Candy Mountain.

Exercise 4 Answers

1. Fairies, little creatures with wings, are not ghosts.
2. Ghosts, like Casper and my Grandpa, are not lemurs.
3. Lemurs, ugly monkeys, are not dogs.
4. Dogs, bow-wow, are not cats.
5. Cats, which are stupid, are not muffins.
6. Those muffins, the blueberry ones, are not yours.

Exercise 5 Answers

1. ~~"The oranges are a beautiful shade of burgundy", Dum-dum said.~~
2. "No, they are not," I said.
3. ~~"Yes, they are", Dum-Dum said.~~
4. "Don't be a sludgeface," I said.
5. ~~"Just look at them", said Dum-Dum. "Those are magical oranges."~~
6. ~~"Oh", I said. "What makes them magical?"~~
7. ~~"They're red,".~~

Exercise 6 Answers

1. You know how the pixies feel about stealing, Meg.
2. I mean, Meg, do you even remember what happened last time?
3. Meg, they made you drink maple syrup for seven years.

4. That was almost as terrible as that movie Seven Years in Tibet.
5. You're right, Meg; Brad Pitt did make that movie a little better.
6. But please, for the love of butter, stop stealing my candy corn waffles.

Exercise 7 Answers

1. I ride a quick, fast broomstick.
2. I own 50 turquoise owls.
3. I make delicious, tasty Nutter Beer.
4. I wish I owned a magical red hippogriff.

Exercise 8 Answers

Completed Exercise (filled in by Bob Ristau)

When I went to the **Lollipop Castle**, I bought a **box of artichoke hearts**. Clearly, they were made by **Gigantosaurs** and not intended for human consumption. The cashier warned me, "Bro, that stuff's nasty." But I did not **harken**, and I feasted on them **slovenly**. They tasted **pasty, parabolic**, and **translucent**. On May **17, 2015,** I died of **gangrene**. That day, a very **swollen** day indeed, was the end of my existence as a human. That's cool, though. Now, I'm a **manticore**.

Ristau & Anderson

Glossary

AAAWWUBBIS – As, After, Although, While, When, Until, Before, Because, If and Since. If you add one of these subordinating conjunctions onto a clause, that clause won't be able to stand on its own without some help.

Adjectives: describing words. Use them when you want to insult someone.

Comma – the subject of this book, it is a punctuation mark that looks like a boomerang. Grammar dragons love them. They are like unicorn sprinkles.

Comma splice – when losers use a comma to separate independent clauses without a coordinating conjunction.

Coordinate adjectives: adjectives that describe the same noun in the same way. They need a comma between them or things get nasty. They have too much in common.

Coordinating conjunction – a connector word like: For, And, Nor, But, Or, Yet, and So. They are FANBOYS that bring ideas and unicorns together.

Cumulative adjectives: adjectives that describe the noun in different ways in a particular order. They don't need a comma between them. They're besties. They build off each other.

Dependent clause – a group of words that has both a subject and a predicate but cannot stand on its own as a sentence. It needs some more goodness.

Direct Address – writing that directly speaks to someone, usually with their name. Not with their actual address, though. That would be a bit **stalkerish**.

FANBOYS - the coordinating conjunctions For, And, Nor, But, Or, Yet, and So. Also, boys who lose their voices and gawk at famous people.

Grammar - stuff you forgot.

Independent clause – a group of words that has both a subject and a predicate; it can stand alone as a sentence. It's an independent lady that can't deal with you if you too shaky.

Metaphor – a fancy excuse to make weird comparisons.

Nonrestrictive – a phrase, clause or idea that you could delete from the sentence, and your mom wouldn't notice.

Nouns – a person, place, thing, idea, or animal. My soul is a noun – it is a thing. Your soul is also a noun, even though it is an idea. Also, sorry your soul got eaten by that manticore.

Oxford Comma – the civilized comma that appears before the *and* in a list. Spangle hates it.

Predicate – the part of the sentence that tells us something about the subject (like what it is doing or being). It kinda sounds like pretty cat.

Righteous – a higher plane of awesomeness. Often achieved by my mom and nonrestrictives.

Sasquatch – also known as Bigfoot, sasquatch is a large, hairy creature capable of immense tenderness. Plus, sasquatch loves hugs and filling.

Sentence Fragment – a sentence that is incomplete. It is either missing a subject or a predicate (or both). It may also be missing a soul.

Stalkerish – not actually a word. It is word-ish.

Subject – who or what the sentence is about. Also, Math and History.

Transitions – connect words and ideas like little troll bridges. Only without the trolls. And probably cuter.

Troll – an ugly, slow-witted creature that does not use the Oxford Comma.

Ristau & Anderson

The Authors

Kate Ristau is an author and an instructor at Western Oregon University. She grew up hating commas, but has now grown to love them. Sometimes she dreams about them when she is not thinking about more important things (like dragons, unicorns, and fairies). Her work focuses on folklore, magic, and myth, and if she had it her way, she would drink a lot more coffee and write a lot more books. She lives with her husband, her son, and her dog in Portland, Oregon. If you can't find her there, you can find her at www.kateristau.com.

Maren Bradley Anderson is a writer, teacher, podcaster, blogger, and alpaca rancher who lives in the Willamette Valley of Oregon. She worries about comma abuse at times, but has stopped short of making a public service announcement for television. She teaches literature and writing at Western Oregon University and blogs about alpacas and writing. Her alpacas win ribbons, and she thinks they are darned cute. She lives with her husband, children, and a barnful of animals. You can find her at www.marens.com.

Made in the USA
San Bernardino, CA
05 March 2016